# A~Z of unusual words
# *JOBS* and
# *HOBBIES*

### Written by Sue Finnie
### Illustrated by James Alexander

Woodbridge, England *Publishing*

### Actuary
A person who deals with financial matters. For example, an actuary might work for an insurance company working out risk values and calculating what people should pay for their insurance

### Acupuncturist
Healer who uses needles, electrical stimulators or small cones of burning herbs to stimulate special points in the body to keep patients healthy

### Administrator
An organiser, especially in business or government affairs, who manages people and resources

### Advocate
Someone who gives legal advice and presents cases in court on behalf of a client

### Aeronautical Engineer
A person who designs, tests and builds aircraft

### Ag-Pilot
Someone who flies a helicopter or plane low over agricultural land and sprays crops with fertiliser or other chemicals

### Agony Aunt
A woman (or man!) who works for a newspaper, magazine or TV/radio programme advising people on how to cope with their personal problems

### Agricultural Engineer
Someone who designs, develops and makes agricultural equipment or buildings

### Agronomist
An expert in field crop production and soil management

### Air Traffic Controller
The person who directs and controls the movement of planes while they are in the air and at the airport. Air traffic controllers use radar and radio equipment to make sure all planes are a safe distance apart

### Anaesthetist
A medical specialist who gives patients an anaesthetic to make them unconscious before an operation

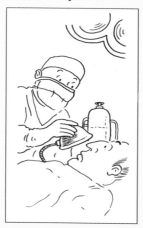

### Angler
A person whose hobby is fishing

### Animator
An artist who draws cartoons for films

### Anthropologist
A scientist who studies human beings. Anthropologists are especially interested in anything to do with race, culture or relationships in different societies

### Antiquarian
Anyone who studies or collects antiquities, usually objects which date from before the Middle Ages

### Antiquarian Bookseller
A shopkeeper who sells old and rare books, manuscripts, etchings, etc.

### Antiquary
A person who collects, deals in or studies antiques, ancient works of art or ancient times

### Antique Dealer
Someone who buys and sells antiques, such as works of art, furniture or ornaments

## Apiarist
Someone who keeps bees, either as a job or for a hobby

## Apprentice
A young person learning a job, usually a manual trade

## Aquaculturalist
A person who cultivates plants and animals that live in water to be eaten or used by human beings

## Aquanaut
A person who works, swimming or diving, underwater

## Aquarist
An enthusiast who keeps fish, usually in tanks

## Arboriculturalist
An expert on trees, how they grow and how to look after them

## Archbishop
The chief bishop in a city area

## Archeologist
A scientist who learns about how people used to live in the past by studying ancient objects

## Architect
A designer who draws plans of buildings and makes sure they are properly built

## Archivist
The keeper of records, manuscripts and documents of historical importance

## Arms Dealer
A person who buys, sells and transports guns and other weapons

## Aromatherapist
A person who uses the aroma (smells) from oils and balms to relieve stress and make people feel better

**Astrobiologist**
A biologist who investigates the possibility of life on other planets

**Astrologer**
Someone who interprets the position of the planets, the sun and the moon to give information about people's lives and characters

**Astronaut**
A person trained to travel in Space

**Astronomer**
A scientist who studies the planets and the universe as a whole

**Astrophysicist**
An astronomer who is interested in the physical and chemical make-up of planets

**Attorney**
A lawyer who represents clients in legal proceedings

**Au Pair**
A young foreigner who lives temporarily with a family abroad, usually doing housework or looking after children in exchange for pocket money and board and lodging

**Auctioneer**
Person who conducts an auction sale, either in an auction room, on site or in a market

**Audiological Scientist**
A scientist who tests people's hearing and who develops hearing aids and other equipment to help people with hearing problems

# A

**Auditor**
A person who examines the accounts of a business to make sure they are in order

**Auteur**
A film director, especially one who is very creative

**Author**
A writer, usually of books

**Autobiographer**
A person who has written his/her own life story

**Aviculturalist**
Someone who keeps and breeds birds

# B

**Bailiff**
1. An officer of the law who serves writs, makes arrests, etc.
2. A person who works for a landlord or landowner, perhaps managing a farm or patrolling fishing waters

**Ballboy or girl**
The boy or girl who fetches balls that go out of play at a sports match (tennis, rugby, football, etc.)

**Ballet Shoemaker**
A cobbler who makes each ballet shoe by hand. A professional ballerina can wear out two pairs of ballet shoes in a single performance!

**Balloonist**
The pilot of a hot air balloon

**Balneologist**
A person with a knowledge of the branch of science called balneology (how baths, especially in natural mineral waters, can help relieve and cure aches and pains and diseases)

**Band Roadie**
The person responsible for looking after the equipment, transport and other practical arrangements of bands and groups when they go on tour

**Bank Teller**
A person who works in a bank, dealing with people at the counter. Tellers take in and pay out money

**Banker Mason**
Someone who works in a workshop or stoneyard cutting and shaping stone blocks

**Barrister (-at-Law)**
Someone who gives legal advice and presents cases in court on behalf of clients

**Beautician**
A person who provides beauty treatments to make other people look more attractive or beautiful

**Beefeater**
The popular name for a Yeoman of the Guard or a Yeoman Warder at the Tower of London

**Bellboy or Bellhop**
A boy who works in a hotel carrying luggage, operating lifts, opening doors and so on

# B

### Biathlete
A sportsperson who competes in the Biathlon, a cross-country skiing race broken up with target shooting

### Bill Poster
Someone who fixes posters to advertising hoardings. Large posters come in ready-pasted sections and have to be matched and fitted together carefully

### Biographer
A writer who writes books telling the life stories of other people

### Biologist
A scientist who is interested in the life processes of living things (plants and animals)

### Bishop
A clergyman in charge of a diocese (a number of church areas)

### Blacksmith
A specialist who works iron, especially using a hammer, anvil and furnace

### Bobsleigher
One of a two- or four-person bobsleigh team. Bobsleigh is a winter sport, where teams in an aerodynamic sledge race against the clock down a fast and steep sheer ice course

### Body-Builder
A person who develops the muscles in his/her body through training and special exercises, most often using weights

### Boffin
An expert scientist, usually involved in research

### Bohemian
A person, often an artist or a writer, who lives an unconventional life

**Bookie**
A popular name for a 'bookmaker'

**Bookkeeper**
The person who keeps regular records of transactions in a business, or who keeps accounts

**Bookmaker**
Someone who takes bets, especially on horse races

**Botanist**
A scientist who studies plants and plant life

**Bouncer**
A person (usually large!) whose job is to keep order at a nightclub, dance, etc.

**Brewer**
Someone who makes beer or ale by the process of brewing

**Broker**
A person who acts on someone else's behalf in a business deal

**Bureaucrat**
Usually a government official, but sometimes a name given to an office-worker

**Busker**
A street musician who plays and collects money from passers-by

**Bow Maker**
Person who makes and repairs bows for stringed musical instruments, like violins, usually from exotic woods and horsehair

**Butler**
1. The chief male servant in a rich household
2. A manservant who looks after wines and spirits

# C

**Calligrapher**
An artist who uses calligraphy (decorative handwriting) for special documents

**Campanologist**
Person who rings bells as a hobby

**Cardiologist**
A medical specialist who does tests on a patient's heart

**Care Assistant**
A person who helps to look after children, old people or the handicapped in a residential home or day centre

**Carpenter**
A person who makes (or repairs) things from wood

**Cartographer**
Someone who makes maps

**Cartoonist**
An artist who draws caricatures of people or animals, usually humorous

**Casting Director**
The person whose job it is to suggest suitable actors and actresses to hire for the different parts in a film or TV production

**Chancellor of the Exchequer**
A senior government minister who looks after matters relating to money, the economy and so on

**Chandler**
Originally a chandler was a person who made and sold candles. Nowadays it's anyone who sells a specific type of goods. For example, a ship's chandler sells things used on ships

### Chargehand
Person in charge of a group of manual workers

### Chartered Surveyor
A person who carefully inspects property and land and sets a value on it

### Chauffeur
Someone who drives a car for other people, usually an organisation or a wealthy person. Chauffeurs often wear a uniform

### Chef
A cook, especially the head cook in a restaurant

### Chiropodist
A specialist in foot care. Chiropodists help people keep their feet healthy by inspecting them, advising on footwear and offering treatment (massage, exercises, drugs, surgery, etc.)

### Chiropractor
A healer who massages and manipulates his/her patient's body to adjust the structure of their body. Chiropractors often treat people with back-ache

### Choreographer
The person who makes up and teaches dance routines for a show or other type of performance

### Civil Servant
Someone who works for the State and whose wages are paid out of taxpayers' money

# C

**Clairvoyant**
Someone who claims they have the power to see into the future

**Clergyman**
A person in the church who has taken holy orders

**Clerical Worker**
Anyone who works in an office following a routine or in administration

**Clerk**
1. Somebody who keeps accounts or records, usually an office worker
2. A member of the clergy

**Clerk of Works**
A specialist who makes sure builders or workers are following plans

**Coach**
An instructor who helps others to develop their sporting or academic skills

**Coachbuilder**
Someone who restores old cars by straightening out dents in the bodywork or producing new replacement panels, particularly after accidents

**Coastguard**
Someone who works near the sea and not only rescues those in trouble at sea but also watches clifftops, keeps a look-out for smugglers, etc.

**Cobbler**
The maker or mender of things made from leather, usually shoes

**Codicologist**
A person who studies manuscripts

**Commando**
A soldier in a unit which carries out surprise raids

**Commercial Traveller**
A salesperson who travels round a region selling to customers and getting new business

**Commis**
An apprentice waiter or chef

**Commissaire**
A referee in professional cycle racing who travels in an open-topped car with the riders to make sure no-one breaks the rules

**Commissionaire**
A uniformed doorman at a hotel or theatre

**Commodity Dealer**
A dealer who buys and sells metals and raw materials for clients all over the world

**Compere**
The presenter of a TV/radio programme or show, who introduces the acts

**Computer Operator**
A computer person who writes special programs for a computer so that it will perform different tasks

**Conchologist**
A person who collects shells, usually as a hobby

**Conductor**
1. Leader of an orchestra who stands in the front and uses a baton to direct the musicians

2. Someone who sells and checks tickets on a bus, train, etc.

**Conjurer**
A person who performs tricks using illusions or very swift movements

# C

### Conservationist
Anyone who, as a job or hobby, tries to protect nature from harmful change

### Cooper
Craftsperson who makes or repairs wooden barrels or casks

### Copytaster
On a newspaper, the person who looks at the news when it first comes in and decides whether or not it is worth including

### Copywriter
Man or woman who works for an advertising agency writing the words for advertisements

### Coroner
The person who tries to find out why someone died if the cause of death is at all suspicious

### Cosmetician
A person who makes, sells or applies cosmetics (make-up)

### Councillor
A member of a local Council; the District, County or Regional equivalent of a Member of Parliament

### Counsellor
Someone who offers help and advice to people with problems

### Countryside Ranger
An employee who looks after the environment and the countryside by protecting wildlife and encouraging and educating people to act in a responsible way

### Couturier
Fashion designer who makes high-class women's clothes

### Crofter
A farmer who farms a small piece of ground, especially in Northern England and Scotland

D

## Croupier
A casino worker who runs a gambling game like roulette or blackjack

## Customs Officer
Someone who checks goods arriving from another country. Customs officers make sure the proper taxes and tolls are paid and try to stop illegal goods (such as drugs) being smuggled into their country

## Data Inputter
A keyboard operator who puts into a computer information which will be used later for statistics or decision-making

## Decathlete
An athlete who competes in the decathlon, a competition consisting of ten events (running, throwing and jumping)

## Deltiologist
Someone who collects and studies picture postcards, usually as a hobby

## Demolition Worker
A worker who uses tools or machinery (or sometimes explosives) to knock down buildings and then clears the site

# D

**Denrochronologist**
A person who studies the rings of tree trunks, particularly in order to pinpoint the date of past events

**Dermatologist**
A medical specialist who deals with diseases of the skin

**Diarist**
A person who keeps a diary and sometimes writes for a newspaper or magazine

**Dietician**
Someone who plans and gives advice on special diets and helps people to eat sensibly

**Dog Handler**
A member of the police or armed forces who trains and looks after dogs which do special work, such as mountain rescue or sniffing out bombs or drugs

**Dog Warden**
A person, usually employed by a local council, who deals with stray dogs and teaches people how to look after their dogs

**Don**
1. A head, tutor or fellow in one of the colleges that make up Oxford and Cambridge Universities
2. A general word for a university teacher

**Doxographer**
A person who collects the opinions of ancient Greek philosophers by reading their writings

**Draper**
Someone who sells cloth, clothing and soft furnishings

**Draughtsperson**
An artist who draws plans of buildings or machinery

# E

**Ecologist**
A scientist who studies living things and the environment they live in

**Economist**
A person who studies the economy (society and resources)

**Editor**
1. The person who edits (prepares) written material before it is published
2. The person who decides which articles will go into a newspaper, magazine or TV/radio programme

**Embalmer**
Someone who prepares dead bodies that are waiting to be buried or cremated

**Environmental Health Officer**
A person responsible for making sure that living and working conditions in the community are healthy

**Environmentalist**
A person who cares about the environment and living things and often warn of dangers that can damage the environment

**Equerry**
1. An officer who looks after horses for a prince or nobleman
2. An officer who personally attends a member of the British Royal family

**Equestrienne**
A female horseback rider, especially in a circus

**Escapologist**
A person who, usually to entertain others, escapes from chains, ropes or locked containers

**Estate Agent**
Someone who acts on behalf of people who are buying, selling or renting out property or land

## E

**Etymologist**
A historian interested in the origins of words and the way they have developed

## F

**Factotum**
A servant who does lots of different jobs

**Falconer**
A breeder or trainer of hawks, or a person who uses hawks for hunting

**Farrier**
1. A horse doctor
2. A blacksmith who shoes horses

**Felon**
A criminal

**Film Editor**
The person who chooses and arranges individual shots in order to build up a sequence for a film

**Flautist**
A musician who plays the flute

**Fletcher**
A person who makes arrows to be used in archery

**Floor Manager**
A person who works in a theatre or studio and is responsible for dealing with scenery, cameras and other equipment

**Flunky (or Flunkey)**
1. A servant in uniform.
2. A slang word for a 'hanger-on'

**Forensic Scientist**
An expert who helps police detectives by examining evidence found at the scene of a crime. Even a trace of blood, paint or soil or a single hair can provide valuable clues

**Fortune Teller**
A person who claims to have the power to read other people's futures from tea leaves, cards, etc.

**Freestylist**
A sportsperson who does not follow a set style, but chooses their own style in a freestyle event

## French Polisher
A craftsperson who gets a smooth, highly-polished surface finish to wood by patient sanding, colouring, rubbing and applying French polish

## Front-of-House Manager
The person in charge of all the staff who work in the parts of a theatre used by the audience

## Funambulist
A tightrope walker

## Funeral Director
A person who arranges funerals

## Furrier
A dealer in fur

## Gaffer
1. Chief lighting electrician in a film or television studio
2. A foreman in charge of a group of workmen

## Game Show Host/Hostess
The person who presents a TV or radio game show, introduces the guests, asks questions and explains how the game is played

## Ganger
The foreman in charge of a gang of labourers

## Genealogist
Anyone who traces family histories, either as a job or for fun

# G

### General Practitioner (or G.P.)
A doctor who is not based in a hospital but who has a practice in a local community. Your GP is normally the first person you go to see when you are ill

### Geneticist
A person who works in medicine or agriculture, usually doing research, who studies inherited characteristics in people, animals or plants

### Geriatrician
A medical specialist who deals with the problems of old people

### Ghillie (sometimes Gillie)
In Scotland, a local person who looks after someone who has paid to hunt or fish

### Ghost Writer
A writer who writes articles or books in the name of someone else. Famous people often use ghost writers to help them write books

### Girl Friday
Usually an office-worker who can turn her hand to lots of different jobs

### Glazier
Someone who cuts and fits glass, usually for windows

### Graphic Designer
An artist who plans layouts and draws illustrations for books, magazines, publicity or any other printed material

### Graphologist
An expert in handwriting, especially in what handwriting tells about the writer's character

### Grip
A person in a theatre, film or TV studio who handles scenery, lighting, props or camera equipment

### Groundsman
A specialist who marks out and looks after sports pitches

### Haberdasher
Someone who sells buttons, thread, ribbons and other things used for making clothes

### Hacker
A person who uses a personal computer to break into the computer system of a government, organisation, etc.

### Hagiographer
A writer who writes about the lives of saints

### Handyman
A manual worker who can do most kinds of small jobs

### Hang Glider
A person who hangs from a frame covered in canvas and who flies, being carried along by air currents

### Harbourmaster
The person in charge of a harbour or port who is responsible for the coming and going of ships

### Harpist
A musician who plays the harp

### Hawker
Anyone who tries to sell things in the street or by knocking at front doors trying to sell

# H

## Helmsman
Member of the crew of a ship or yacht who steers

## Heptathlete
An athlete who competes in the Heptathlon, a women's competition involving seven running, jumping and throwing events

## Herbalist
A person who grows or sells herbs, especially for use as medicines

## HGV Driver
Driver of a large lorry. HGV stands for 'Heavy Goods Vehicle' and you need a special HGV licence before you are allowed to drive one

## Historian
Someone who studies or writes about history

## Historiographer
Someone who writes an official history, of royalty or a regiment, for example

## Hod Carrier
A worker on a building site who uses a hod to carry bricks. A hod is made of wood, shaped like a 'V', on the end of a pole

## Homeopath
An expert in natural remedies who treats patients with small doses designed to stimulate the body's own healing powers

## Horologer (or Horologist)
1. A person who makes clocks, watches and other instruments for measuring time
2. A person involved in the science of measuring time

## Horticulturalist
A person whose job is to grow, fruit, vegetables or flowers

### Hydrographic Surveyor
Someone who does surveys of rivers, harbours and the seabed which can be used when making nautical charts

### Hydrologist
A person who studies the distribution of the water of the earth and its atmosphere and how to conserve and use it

### Hydroponicist
A person who grows plants in water with chemical substances added, instead of in soil

### Hydrotherapist
A medical specialist who uses water to treat diseases. Patients often have to bathe or exercise in water containing special chemical substances

### Hyetographer
A person who studies rainfall, e.g. where rain falls and when, and the different ways of recording rainfall

### Hypnologist
A person who studies sleep and hypnosis

### Hypnotist
A person who can make others go into a sleep-like trance in order to reach the deeper parts of their mind

### Illusionist
A sort of magician who makes things appear or disappear - or at least makes it seem as though they have

### Illustrator
An artist who draws pictures for books, magazines, brochures, etc.

# I

**Impressario**
1. Organiser or sponsor of a large event, such as a concert or sporting event
2. Manager or conductor of an opera or concert company

**Indexer**
A person who prepares indexes for books

**International**
A sportsperson who has represented their country in international competition

**Interpreter**
A person who can speak more than one language and who helps people to communicate at international conferences or during visits abroad by explaining to someone in their own language what has just been said in another language

# J

**Janitor**
Caretaker or doorperson, usually of a school

**Jockey**
Someone who rides horses in races

**Journalist**
A writer who works for a newspaper, magazine or radio or television, usually reporting news

**Journeyman**
A person who has learned a trade but is employed by another person

**Juror**
1. A member of a jury
2. Someone who takes an oath

**K**

**Keyboardist**
1. A musician who plays a piano, organ or some other instrument with keys
2. A person who operates a typewriter or word processor

**Keynote Speaker**
A speaker (at a conference or seminar, for example) who gives the main speech

**Kissagram man/girl**
A person ( not the shy type!) who is paid to show up at parties or celebrations, usually wearing a fancy costume, and kiss the person celebrating

**Knacker**
1. Somebody who buys old horses for slaughter
2. Somebody who buys old cars, ships, houses, etc. in order to break them up and sell off the parts

**Labourer**
Someone who does physical work, usually unskilled

**Laird**
Lord of the Manor in Scotland

**Landlady/Landlord**
1. Someone who owns or manages a pub
2. Someone who owns a property which is rented out to other people

**Landscape Architect**
A person who draws up plans for land development, which could be anything from gardens and parks to motorways

**Lepidopterist**
Someone who studies or knows a lot about insects, especially moths and butterflies

**Lexicographer**
Someone who writes or edits a dictionary

# L

**Linguist**
A person who speaks, writes and understands (usually) several languages

**Literary Agent**
A person who works for one or more authors, finding publishers to publish their work and negotiating the best possible terms for them. The agent takes a percentage of the author's earnings in payment for this help

**Locum**
A person who stands in for a full-time worker, such as a doctor, when they are absent (on holiday or off sick, for example)

# M

**Managing Director**
The boss of a company who has overall control of other directors and departments

**Manicurist**
A person who treats other people's hands and fingernails to make them look attractive and keep them healthy

**Marine Biologist**
A biologist who studies things that live in the sea

**Market Researcher**
Someone who studies how customers behave, what they want and what influences them

**Marketing Manager**
The manager responsible for interesting customers in a product and for getting the goods to them

### Masher
The worker who supervises or carries out grain-crushing in the making of spirits such as whisky

### Masseur/Masseuse
A man or woman who relieves the aches and pains of others by rubbing parts of their body with their hands

### Master of Ceremonies (or M.C.)
A speaker who introduces events or performers

### Matador
A bullfighter who has the main role at a bullfight. It is the matador who kills the bull

### Mayor
The head of a local city or borough council in England or Wales

### Medium
Anyone who claims that they can can get in contact with the spirits of dead people and communicate with them, usually on behalf of someone else, such as a friend or relative of the dead person

### Mentor
A loyal and wise adviser

### Mercenary
A person who is hired to fight for a foreign army. A mercenary fights only to earn money, not because he believes in the cause

### Meteorologist
The person who works out the weather forecasts we hear on the radio or television or read in the newspaper

## Microbiologist
A scientist who studies micro-organisms (viruses, bacteria, etc.) using a microscope. Microbiologists are often experts in plant or animal diseases

## Microlight Pilot
A pilot who flies microlight aircraft (light flying frames with small engines)

## Midwife
A nurse who delivers babies and who looks after mothers before, during and after the birth

## Milliner
Someone who designs, makes and sells hats

## Minister
1. A member of the government who is the head of a government department
2. A person who has taken holy orders and is in charge of a church, conducts religious services, etc.

## Missionary
A person who works in a mission, especially a religious mission taking religious faith to new territories

## Mixer
Short for SOUND MIXER or VISION MIXER

## Mobster
Member of a gang of criminals

## Monk
A man who lives in a religious community and has made vows dedicating his life to God

## Morris Dancer
A traditional English folk dancer who wears a special costume with knee-straps with small bells attached

## Mortician
An undertaker or funeral director

**Mortuary Attendant**
Person who works in a mortuary, the place where bodies are kept until they are buried or cremated

**Mountaineer**
A person who climbs high hills and mountains

**Muezzin**
The official of a mosque (where Muslim people worship) who calls the faithful to prayer five times a day

**Nanny**
Person who looks after other people's babies and children, usually while the parents are out at work

**Nark**
An informer or spy, especially one who works for the police

**Navigator**
A crew membe (ship, aircraft or motor vehicle) who uses maps, charts, compasses or sextants to plot the route to a destination

**Netminder**
The goalkeeper in Ice Hockey

**Neurosurgeon**
A surgeon who treats disorders of the nervous system

**Notary**
A writer who draws up oaths and other legal documents

**Novelist**
An author who writes novels

**Numismatist**
A collector of coins, paper money, tokens, medals, etc.

**Nun**
A woman who lives in a convent and has made vows dedicating her life to God

**Nurseryman**
A person who owns or works in a nursery where plants are grown

## N

**Nutritionist**
An advisor who tells others what food to eat to stay healthy, especially if they have medical problems

## O

**Oceanographer**
Someone who studies and knows about oceans

**Ocularist**
Someone who makes and fits artificial eyes

**Occupational Therapist**
A specialist who helps people to recover from illnesses or accidents by organising creative activities for them

**Odd-job Man**
A manual worker who will do all sorts of small jobs

**Oncologist**
A medical specialist who identifies and treats tumours

**One-man Band**
1. A musician who plays several instruments at the same time (some may have to be carefully balanced or tied on)

2. Someone in business who does everything him/herself

**Ophiologist**
A zoologist who studies snakes

**Opthalmic Optician**
see Optometrist

**Optician**
A specialist who tests eyes and prescribes spectacles or contact lenses to help people see better

### Optometrist
A specialist who tests people's sight, measures defects in their vision and prescribes spectacles or contact lenses. An optometrist does not treat diseases of the eye but refers patients to a doctor when necessary

### Orthodontist
A dentist who specialises in straightening out irregular teeth

### Orthopaedic Surgeon
A surgeon who specialises in treating bones and muscles that are broken or deformed

### Orthoptist
Specialist who can diagnose and treat defects in the muscles of the eye

**P**

### Packaging Technologist
A person whose job is to improve the way packaging is designed and produced, making sure it is safe, clean, easy to use, attractive, etc.

### Paediatrician
A hospital doctor who is an expert in children's illnesses

### Page
1. A boy who takes messages or runs errands
2. A boy who attends the bride at a wedding

### Palaeontologist
A scientist who studies fossils to find out about life in the past

### Palaeographer
An expert in ancient writing and inscriptions

### Palaeozoologist
Also known as Palaeotologist. A person who studies fossil animals

### Palmist
Someone who claims to be able to tell other people's fortunes by studying the lines in the skin on the palms of their hands

### Panelbeater
A worker who straightens out bumps and dents in the metal panels that make up cars and other vehicles, after accidents

### Paramedic
A person, such as a laboratory technician, who helps doctors in their work

### Paratrooper
A soldier trained and equipped to parachute out of an aeroplane into a battle area

### Park Ranger (or Park Keeper)
A person who works in a park and who is responsible for security, keeping order and helping visitors

### Pathologist
A medical specialist who carries out tests (postmortems) on dead bodies to find out the cause of death

### Percussionist
Member of an orchestra who plays a percussion instrument (drums, cymbals, etc.)

### Peripatetic Teacher
A teacher who moves around teaching in a number of different schools in the course of a week

### Perruquier
A wigmaker

### Personnel Manager
The person who is responsible for all jobs relating to the employment of staff within an organisation, such as recruitment, training, wages, health and safety of workers, etc.

**Pest Controller**
Someone who finds and gets rid of rats, insects and other pests which might be a danger to health or do damage to crops or foodstuffs

**Pharmacist**
A chemist who supplies people with drugs and medicines which have been prescribed by the doctor. An industrial pharmacist works on the production of drugs and medicines

**Pharmacologist**
A scientist who studies the effects of drugs and chemicals on humans and animals

**Philanthropist**
A person, usually rich, who is kind to others and who gives money to good causes

**Philatelist**
A collector of postage stamps

**Phillumenist**
A person who collects matchbox labels

**Philosopher**
Someone who studies philosophy, ways of life and wisdom

**Phoneticist**
An expert in the sounds of speech

**Physicist**
A scientist who studies matter and energy, including mechanics, heat, electricity and atomic structure

**Physiotherapist**
Someone trained to treat injuries or illnesses through exercise or massage

**Picture Restorer**
A person who cleans paintings and restores them to their original beauty by patching and repairing them

### Pigeon Fancier
A person who breeds and/or races pigeons

### Pisciculturalist
A person who rears fish. A fish farmer

### Poet Laureate
A great poet who has been appointed as a lifetime officer of the British royal household

### Politician
A person actively involved in politics

### Poultry Hand
Farm worker who rears hens to produce eggs or for sale as food

### Prima Ballerina
A leading female ballet dancer

### Producer
The person responsible for getting a performance (play, film, TV or radio programme, for example) put on properly

### Professor
Head of a University department who teaches and does research into a subject

### Proof Reader
Someone who works for a publisher or printer checking proofs (drafts of the text to be printed). Proof readers must check that the printed version is the same as the original and mark any mistakes before the text is printed

### Propagator
A gardener who grows new plants from cuttings taken from a parent plant

### Provost
1. Scottish version of a mayor
2. Official who works in a cathedral

### PSV Driver
Usually a bus driver. PSV stands for 'Public Service Vehicle' and you need a special PSV licence before you are allowed to drive one

### Psychiatrist
A medical specialist who treats people who have mental, emotional or behavioural problems

### Psychic
Someone who can feel supernatural forces

### Psychoanalyst
Someone who helps people with mental and emotional problems by investigating their unconscious mind

### Psychogeriatrician
A medical specialist involved with the health care of old people with mental disorders

### Psychologist
A person who makes a scientific study of human behaviour. Some psychologists work in hospitals helping to treat patients with mental disorders, others help children with learning problems or study people at work

### Publican
The owner or manager of a pub or other premises licensed to sell alcohol

### Pugilist
Another name for a boxer

### Quack
Usually someone who says they are a doctor when they have no appropriate qualifications. Can be anyone who claims to be a professional without proof of their qualifications and ability

### Quantity Surveyor
Someone who works out how much material (e.g. wood, bricks) will be needed for building something

# R

### Rabbi
The minister of a synagogue (where Jewish people worship)

### Radiographer
A hospital worker who operates X-ray equipment

### Radiologist
A medical specialist who uses radiant energy (like X-rays and gamma rays) to treat and cure disease

### Radiotherapist
A medical specialist who uses radiation and radio

### Receiver
The person whose job is to wind up a business that has gone bankrupt

### Receptionist
The person who greets and receives visitors to an organisation (like a hotel, an office or a doctor's surgery), answers the telephone and makes appointments

### Referee
1. A person who makes sure players stick to the rules in a sports contest
2. Someone who is asked to give information about the character and ability of a person applying for a job

### Reporter
1. A journalist for a newspaper, television or radio who reports on news stories

2. Someone who keeps a record of a meeting in shorthand

### Reprographer
Someone who reproduces or makes copies of printed material

### Researcher
Sometimes called a Research Assistant. A person whose job is to discover and present facts, theories, etc. Researchers work in different fields - industry, medicine, the media, business, etc.

### Rights Manager
In a publishing company , the person who sells rights in a book to other companies ( for example, the right to translate the book into another language or the right to make a TV programme or film based on it)

### Roustabout
Worker on an oil rig who helps with general labouring jobs, loading and stacking equipment or setting up machinery, for example

### Runner
1. Someone who acts as a messenger for a bank, stockbroker or newspaper
2. A person who runs between the wickets for an injured batsman in cricket

### Sailmaker
The designer or maker of sails for boats

### Sapper
A soldier in the Royal Engineers (who build and look after specialised equipment)

### Saw Doctor
Worker in a sawmill who keeps the saws in good working order

### Scaffolder
Worker who fits together the metal scaffolding which construction workers use when working on buildings high above the ground

**Scratch Golfer**
A golf player who is good enough not to need a handicap and who would be expected to score par or better

**Script Writer**
A writer who writes scripts for radio or television programmes (comedies, drama, chat shows, etc.)

**Scrivener**
A writer who draws up documents, usually legal

**Scuba Diver**
A diver who uses an aqualung or bottled air to help him/her breathe

**Sergeant-at-arms**
An officer who attends the Speaker in Parliament, or the Lord Chancellor, who is responsible for keeping order

**Shepherd**
A person who looks after a flock of sheep. He often works with a trained sheepdog

**Shop Steward**
Local representative of a group of union members who tries to get better working conditions for members or helps them if they have a disagreement with management

**Shot Blaster**
A person who uses high pressure equipment to clean stone or metal surfaces. Shot, or a special mixture of sand, is sprayed onto old buildings to clean them

## Slalomist

A sportsperson who goes down a slope zigzagging round a series of poles, cones or other obstacles without touching them. You might find a slalomist in a canoe, on skis, on roller skates, on a skateboard, etc.

## Sleeping Partner

Someone who has put money into a business but who does not take an active part in running it

## Sociologist

A scientist who studies society, human behaviour and social relationships

## Software Designer/Engineer

The person who writes/produces the programs which make computers operate

## Solicitor

Someone who gives people legal advice, when they are buying or selling a house, getting a divorce or preparing a contract or will for example

## Soloist

A musical performer who sings or plays a musical instrument on their own, with or without backing accompaniment

## Sound Mixer

A technician who mixes together different sounds (like voices, music or sound effects) for a recording or film

## Sound Recordist

A technician who works in a studio making sure that sound levels and recordings are OK

# S

### Sous Chef
An assistant chef, or cook

### Speaker
1. The person who presides over the House of Commons or another law-making body
2. Someone who makes a speech at a conference, dinner, meeting, etc.

### Speech Therapist
A specialist who helps people who have difficulties speaking clearly

### Sporran Maker
A person who makes sporrans (purses worn with kilts as part of the Scottish national dress for men)

### Spy
Someone who has access to information (economic, military or industrial) and who trades it

### Stage Hand
A person in theatre or television who helps the Stage Manager with putting up or shifting scenery, working the curtains and so on

### Stage Manager/Manageress
A member of a theatre company who looks after the stage set, special effects, etc.

### Stalker
The person who leads a group of people who are hunting animals

### Statistician
Someone who collects and analyses information and presents it in the form of statistics, often in charts or diagrams

### Steeplechaser
A rider who races horses over jumps or obstacles

### Steeplejack
A skilled worker (with a head for heights!) who builds and repairs steeples, chimneys, roofs, etc.

### Stenographer
A shorthand typist

### Stevedore
A person who works on the docks, moving cargo either by hand or with equipment

### Stockbroker
A dealer in stocks and shares who advises clients on the best way to invest their money and who buys and sells securities for them on the Stock Exchange

### Stonemason
A craftsperson who works with stone and who can carve lettering on stone

### Stuntman/woman
A person who acts as a stand-in for an actor or actress during the filming of a dangerous or risky scene, like crashing a car or jumping from a height

### Submariner
A crewman on a submarine

### Systems Analyst
A computer person who shows how a manual task will be made into an automated (computer) one

### Tattooer (or Tattooist)
An artist who draws permanent pictures on people's skin, using needles and ink

### Taxidermist
Someone who makes life-like models of animals and birds using an artificial frame and the hide or feathers of a dead animal or bird

### Tegestologist
Someone who collects beer mats, usually as a hobby

### Telephonist
A worker whose job is to answer the phone and pass calls on to the right person

### Telesalesperson
A man or woman who sells something by telephone

### Textile Operative
A person who works at a machine which weaves or knits yarn to make fabric

### Thespian
A rather grand name for an actor or actress

### Three-day Eventer
A horse rider who takes part in a competition which lasts three days. The events are dressage, cross-country and show-jumping

### Toolmaker
A worker who makes the different tools used for production work in a factory

### Topiarist
Someone who trims, cuts and trains trees and bushes into ornamental shapes

### Touch Judge

An official in rugby who helps the referee and who says when and where the ball goes out of play

### Planner

A person who plans how to make the best use of land, particularly in areas where towns are expanding or new towns are being built.

### Toxicologist

A biologist who deals with poisons and their effects, and with any problems they cause (medical or legal problems, for example)

### Toxophilite

An archer, a person who uses a bow and arrow

### Tragedian

A writer who writes tragedy poems or plays (involving death)

### Train Spotter

An enthusiast who, as a hobby, observes and notes down details of trains using train number reference books and timetables

### Translator

A person fluent in more than one language who translates written text from one language to another

### Trapper

A hunter who kills animals in the wild for food or for their fur

## Tree Surgeon

Sometimes called an Arborist or an Arborculturalist. An expert on trees, their health and their care

## Triathlete

A sportsperson who takes part in the Triathlon, a competition consisting of a marathon run, a two-mile swim and a 50-mile cycle race

## Trichologist

Someone who uses scientific techniques to help people who have problems with their hair or scalp, such as baldness, damaged hair or skin irritations

## Tripe Dresser

A butcher who cleans and prepares tripe (cow's stomach), which is a popular food in many European countries

## Trouble Shooter

A name given to someone who has a reputation for being able to solve problems in business

## Turf Accountant

Someone who runs a business which takes bets, especially on horse races. Posh name for a Bookmaker

## Tutor

1. A teacher who teaches one student or a small group of students, looking after their development
2. A private teacher who teaches pupils individually

## Twitcher

A nickname given to a birdwatcher

# U

### Umpire
1. In sport, someone who makes sure that players stick to the rules of the game

2. Someone who gives the final decision on a question or argument

### Undertaker
Another name for a funeral director. An undertaker makes arrangements for the burial or cremation of dead bodies

### Unicyclist
Anyone, often a clown, who rides a one-wheeled cycle

### Upholsterer
Someone who covers furniture frames with padding and fabric to make chairs, sofas, etc.

# V

### VDU Operator
Someone who works at a computer screen or VDU (Visual Display Unit)

### Ventriloquist
A stage performer who holds a dummy (person or animal) and makes it seem as if the dummy is speaking by throwing his/her own voice and working the dummy's mouth

### Verger
A Church official who acts as a caretaker and looks after the inside of a church

### Veterinary Surgeon (or Vet)
A medical specialist who treats animals, especially pets

### Vicar
A person who has taken holy orders and conducts religious services and cares spiritually for the people who go to his church

### Victualler
1. Landlord of a pub, or a publican
2. Someone who provides food for the army or navy, or a ship

### Vintner
A wine merchant

### Virtuoso
A performer whose technique is considered first-rate, usually a musician

### Vision Mixer
A technician who puts together the television signals from cameras, film, etc. to make up a TV programme

### Viticulturalist
Someone who grows grapes to be used for making wine

### Vivisectionist
A scientist who carries out experiments on living animals which involve cutting into the body

### Vocalist
A singer in a band

**Voice-over (Person)**
A person who is not seen on screen but whose voice is heard giving the commentary on a film, TV programme or advert

**Volcanologist**
Someone who studies volcanoes

**Walk-on Actor/Actress**
A person who appears in a play, a film or a TV programme but who does not have a speaking part

**Ward Orderly**
Someone who works in a hospital, doing light cleaning, serving meals and other odd jobs. An orderly has no medical training

**Warden**
A person who looks after the security of people or places (e.g. a youth hostel warden, a prison warden, the warden of an elderly people's home, etc.)

**Wardrobe Mistress**
A member of a theatre or film company who collects, stores, makes and repairs costumes for actors to wear during a production

**Weaver**
Someone who weaves strands of yarn together to make cloth. Wool or cotton can be woven on a loom to make dress fabrics, carpets, rugs etc. Cane is woven by hand to make mats and baskets

**Welder**
A worker who joins metal by heating it to a very high temperature (using electric arc or gas) so that the parts melt together

# W

**Whip**
A Member of Parliament (MP) who directs other people in his/her party how to vote after a debate.

**Wigmaker**
A person who makes wigs or hairpieces

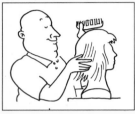

**Window Dresser**
The person who designs and lays out the window displays in a shop

**Witch**
Person who is said to have supernatural powers

**Wood Sawyer**
A worker who sets up and operates power driven saws in a sawmill

# Y

**Yeoman of the Guard**
A soldier who is a bodyguard for the Queen on state occasions

**Yeoman Warder**
One of the guardians of the Tower of London, also called Beefeaters, who wear a special red uniform

# Z

**Zoo Keeper**
Someone who feeds and looks after animals in a zoo

**Zoologist**
A scientist who studies animals and animal life